LAUNCH POINT
Community Group Mission Guide

The Missional Engagement Series

Volume 1
Steps to Faith
Examine Faith • Explore Questions • Encounter God
Where Inquiring Friends Become Solid Disciples

Volume 2
FIRST STEPS Discipleship Training
FIRST STEPS Discipleship Training: Leader's Guide
Turning Newer Believers Into Missional Disciples

Volume 3
Elevate
Experience the Power of Lift
Raising Up Missional Members

Volume 4
Launch Point
Community Group Mission Guide
Moving Small Groups into Mission

LAUNCH POINT
Community Group
Mission Guide

Moving Small Groups into Mission

GARY COMER

VOLUME 4

RESOURCE *Publications* · Eugene, Oregon

LAUNCH POINT
Community Group Mission Guide
Moving Small Groups into Mission, volume 4

The Missional Engagement Series

Copyright © 2014 Gary Comer. All rights reserved. Except for brief quotations in critical publications or reviews, no part of this book may be reproduced in any manner without prior written permission from the publisher. Write: Permissions, Wipf and Stock Publishers, 199 W. 8th Ave., Suite 3, Eugene, OR 97401.

Wipf & Stock
An Imprint of Wipf and Stock Publishers
199 W. 8th Ave., Suite 3
Eugene, OR 97401

www.wipfandstock.com

ISBN 13: 978-1-62032-829-3

Manufactured in the U.S.A.

Scripture taken from the HOLY BIBLE, NEW INTERNATIONAL VERSION®. Copyright © 1973, 1978, 1984 Biblica. Used by permission of Zondervan. All rights reserved.

The "NIV" and "New International Version" trademarks are registered in the United States Patent and Trademark Office by Biblica. Use of either trademark requires the permission of Biblica.

An enormous challenge exists in the church to bridge the pulpit-to-people gap—especially in the area of mission. Fortunately, pastor Dan Zimbardi is a plankbuilder! Not only did he ask me to write this curriculum, but I knew the missional endeavor was important to him, personally. He and his wife, Lori, have invited not-yet-believing neighbors into their home and lives. With mass levels of grace and acceptance offered, people far from God, have found God. For exuding vision and action, I dedicate this course to my dear friend, "Z." May we never forget: The last will be first!

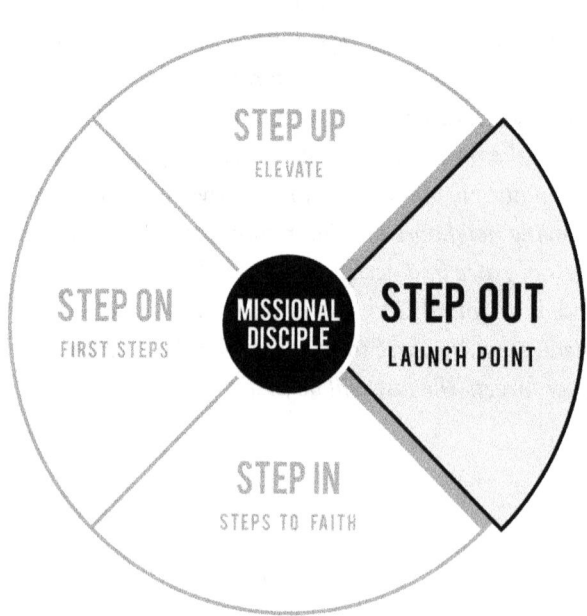

The Missional Engagement Series

Reflected in the hub design, *The Missional Engagement Series* is not one-dimensional or linear, but rather, a holistic layout. Two concepts are critical. First, mission is taught in every phase. Never considered optional or ancillary, being a disciple is about being "on mission" for Jesus. Second, the design develops disciples progressively in stages. By this, it recognizes how Christian maturation actually occurs, needing reinforcement and refinement over time.

Threaded themes drive the curriculum in a compelling way:

Stage	Theme	Description
IN	Invite	Steps to Faith invites not-yet-believers to explore.
ON	Involve	First Steps infuses newer believers with faith practices.
UP	Improve	Elevate raises growth levels in key values.
OUT	Inspire	Launch Point inspires for what God wills to do!

These materials create habits and experiences to shape Christ-likened character and skills. Each vehicle can work independently, yet they fit within a grand design for synergistic impact.

Contents

An Invitation   1

Community Group Mission Guide   3

Week #1—The Soul of Mission   11

Week #2—When Faith is Fantastic   21

Week #3—Learning Faith Formation Process   29

Week #4—Getting Real For the Gospel   41

Week #5—The Gospel and Its Key   49

Week #6—Discerning Belief Barriers   61

Week #7—Coming Home to Jesus   71

Week #8—What Jesus Left Us
        Co-Missioned to Do!   83

Leader's Notes   91

Addendum: Synergistic Mission through
        Community Groups   99

Resources by Gary Comer   101

An Invitation

Being immensely personal, God sometimes communicates in unique and profound ways. On a routine day, this happened to me through an object lesson—I will never forget. Before starting a new position, the senior pastor invited me to a gathering to discuss the disciple making challenge. In my view, this is the most vital and difficult task of the church. Evangelistic mission is not easy, and typically, the weakest link for most Christians. How would we tackle it? I didn't know.

But I knew it was an important meeting and set out plenty early to make it across the freeway with room to spare. Approaching the church building, I was on time. Twenty-minutes early was a minor miracle for someone who presses the margins—like me! As I rolled toward the church, I was feeling good about myself, and felt even better when I had time to delay for the unanticipated train passing. But then something happened. The train stopped. Completely. I sat in my vehicle for ten minutes before anxiously concluding: if I don't do something, I am going to be late!

Forced into action, I boldly maneuvered my truck onto the shoulder and drove backwards past twenty plus lined cars! With no permit or permission I then parked in a company's lot. Abandoning my ride, I got out, walked through the rows of cars only to face the same obstacle of the standstill train. In this moment of bizarre contemplation, I sensed that everyone waiting was now watching. They all wanted to see what I was going to do. I measured how I could crawl underneath, but then saw a ladder, and so I climbed up over the train! As I put my hands to the rails and hoisted myself upward, I had this strange sensation come over me—it was like I was in a movie! What is the line, "Able to leap tall trains in a single bound"—No, it's "tall buildings"—you get the idea—it was invigorating!

Oddly, it was the barrier en route that summoned a message deeper than any idea we could have brainstormed or tallied. God had evoked in me something existential; a profound sense that I was wired intrinsically for adventure. And that he didn't put me on the planet to avoid obstacles, but rather to face those hurdles with whatever courage and creativity I could muster.

It is with this spirit that I am inviting *you* to a very important gathering. Are you ready to discuss your part in the Lord's Great Commission call? To explore with your full facility—what it means to reach this world? And to dive in heart-first for his cause? That is what this workbook is all about. Jesus has much for you to learn and master as his mission emissary. In the Christian life, no challenge is greater—it rises before us!

Yet do not be discouraged or dismayed. "Put your hands to the rails," he whispers. I am laying before you a pathway to a big-time adventure . . . one that will take you on a new course . . . that will lead you to go up and over . . . and that will make you feel totally alive!

1

Community Group Mission Guide

"The Church of God does not have a mission in the world.
The God of mission has a church in the world."

—Tom Dearborne

Undeniably, mission is what makes life an adventure! Though there will always be destinations for you to get to near and far, being missional is not a destination. It is rather an acquired mindset—a mentality with the power to put you smack-dab-in-the-center of God's redemption story! How awesome and humbling is it, to realize that *you* are meant to fill pages in the kingdom's history? Strangely, however, it is often difficult for us to see just how pivotal our role is.

We liken to the stars in J. R. R. Tolkien's epic tale *The Lord of the Rings*, where the future hinges on the unlikeliest of heroes—hobbits: Frodo Baggins, Samwise Gamgee,

Peregrin Took and Meriadoc Brandybuck. Being so small, the races of Middle Earth have overlooked them; and they, too, grapple to comprehend their place. Yet the quest, which they choose to pursue, becomes the greatest adventure of all. At the movie's end, as the four are together hoisting a few beers at the pub, they can barely fathom what they had done.

The idea that our lives serve a greater story is the brilliant insight of J. R. R. Tolkien. A Christian, he knew the battle raging for hearts and minds. He also knew how we strain to see our part. Most of us fail to appreciate how the kingdom's advance actually hinges *on us!* Incredibly, God has delegated the gospel's forward progress. In doing so, he thrusts us into his greatest activity: *Redeeming the world!*

Our Adversary's biggest ploy is to get us to think our part is insignificant or unnecessary. Have you ever found yourself asking, "Is this all that God has for my life?" Ever feel like you don't make a difference or your life does not affect anyone? Lies! Nothing could be further from the truth. Within your calling, you have a role to impact ever-extending networks of relationships. Each person has the potential to grow God's kingdom exponentially. It's often impossible to know what God will do!

Also, like Frodo and his companions, there is something special in the sweet fragrant fellowship when believers link arms for mission goals. As a key member of your church community, this experience awaits you. You will be blessed in working alongside others to expand the

 Gathering together

gospel to a hurting and hungry world. But first you will gather—so that you can get prepared. Are you ready to embark on an amazing course? May the adventure begin!

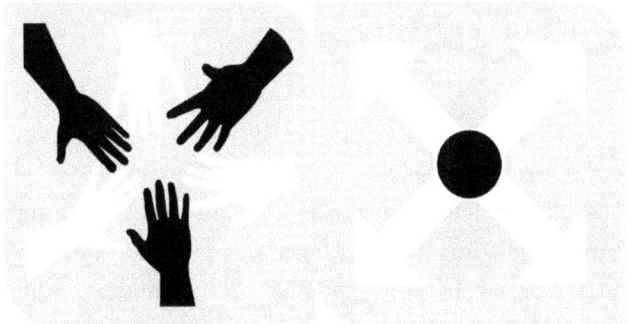

Gathering together   ...for reaching out!

The Goal of This Series

This resource is written for the purpose of guiding *small groups/community groups* to engage in missional activity together and develop disciple making skills. The aim is to lovingly come alongside those outside-the-faith, in order to lead them into belief, community life, and the church. The following graphic depicts the progression of the Community Group/non-believer journey. It begins with relationship, assesses spiritual benefit and barriers, eventually culminating in them following Christ within your community. Notice how the end goal is to produce authentic-on mission disciples!

 **. . . for reaching out!**

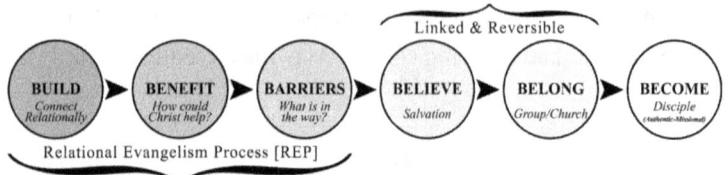

Keep this book with your Bible and bring them every week. Each session will offer direction on how to engage in principle and practice. Both are critical. If a group learned mission principles without practice, the result would be nil. Likewise, practice without understanding spiritual influence principles might not achieve the goal either. Throughout this guide, we will ride both tracks to give us the best chance for influence.

Expectations for What's Ahead!

Let's establish clear expectations for the journey. Practically speaking, each group will:

1. Enter an 8-week study on Jesus's mission patterns.
2. Engage together on fulfilling specific missional assignments.
3. Encourage one another to step out in some new ways!
4. Embrace non-believers relationally, as God opens opportunities, both outside and within group gatherings.
5. Evaluate and celebrate learning and successes!

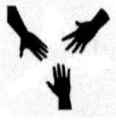 **Gathering together**

In order to provide inspiration to others within the church, it is a good idea to capture the real-life stories on video or through testimony. We want to celebrate what God is doing in reaching our neighborhoods and communities! For those who have made the relational investment to walk another into the faith, we invite you to participate in their baptism. That will be—eternal joy!

Because the eight-weeks builds sequentially and requires focus, the group must commit to the mission. Jesus, himself, was intensely committed to his assignment. Thank God, for us, that he was willing to go the distance! The same principle will apply in reaching your friends. We, too, must realize that a high commitment must match the high challenge. You will have to surrender yourself to pursuing God's will. Remember, God wants to use you and your group to bless others. Be expectant. Allow this training time to take you to new levels of influence!

Dedicating Prayer

Have several pray out for God to meet you in this journey, and to give you the focus and resolve that is necessary.

Session Elements

Now, let's look at the three elements that will guide each session:

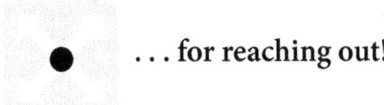

. . . for reaching out!

I. Study:
>Group reading
>Bible passages
>Interactive questions

II. Training:
>Synopsis
>Principle (For emphasis, have the group read it aloud.)
>Group Exercises

III. Engagement:
>Group Sharing: Focus on what God is doing!
>Assignments: Working together inside and outside the session.

Objectives Overview

In the big picture, three major objectives exist. We seek to OIL the mission efforts of the church! Every small group is to:

1. **O**—Organize a community project and possibly other social outreach events as well, as God opens doors for impact.

2. **I**—Invest time relationally with non-believing friends or community contacts.

3. **L**—Learn a relational process of journeying with people all the way into faith.

 **Gathering together**

The sessions will last only eight weeks, but the mission goes on! This series is meant to jumpstart small/community groups toward a mission trajectory. God will then complete what is begun in the months and years ahead!

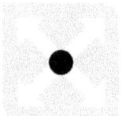 ... for reaching out!

Week #1—BUILD: The Soul of Mission

Please read in preparation for your study:

Don't you love it when someone turns you onto a great flick? Here is my offering to you. *The Snow Walker*. Inspired from the writings of Farley Mowat, it is the adapted story of a self-absorbed American cargo pilot who reluctantly picks up a very sick Eskimo woman and attempts to get her to a hospital. En route the aircraft encounters difficulties and crashes into the frozen tundra of the Alaskan plains.

A survival story ensues, where the young Eskimo woman teaches him not only to survive—but how to live. By the time of her death, this selfish man is transformed. He had taken on more than her skills. Walking alone through blizzard conditions, the final scene fittingly shows him being embraced by an Eskimo community; he had become one of them.

How does God transform us to be like him? This is a great question for a Christian. Magnifying our mission mantle, C. S. Lewis called every Christian to become a "little Christ."[1] In its essence, Christianity is a follower's faith. As Jesus said, "It is enough for students to be like their teacher, and servants like their Master" (Matt 10:24–25). Even though God has gifted teachers within the church, our ultimate discipleship is to Christ himself. Thus, we are to be like him.

In this opening study, we want to take a closer look at what it means to be Christ-like in the fullest sense. Take a moment to read two select passages, and try to discern what these texts have in common.

Read Passages: John 4:31–35; Matthew 9:10–13.

> *[31]Meanwhile his disciples urged him, "Rabbi, eat something." [32]But he said to them, "I have food to eat that you know nothing about." [33]Then his disciples said to each other, "Could someone have brought him food?" [34]"My food," said Jesus, "is to do the will of him who sent me and to finish his work. [35]Do you not say, 'Four months more and then the harvest'? I tell you, open your eyes and look at the fields!*

> *[10]While Jesus was having dinner at Matthew's house, many tax collectors and "sinners" came and ate with him and his disciples. [11]When the Pharisees saw this, they asked his disciples, "Why does your teacher eat with tax collectors and 'sinners'?" [12]On hearing this, Jesus said, "It is not the*

---

1. Lewis, C. S., *Mere Christianity*, New York: Collier/Macmillan, 177.

 **Gathering together**

healthy who need a doctor, but the sick. ¹³But go and learn what this means: 'I desire mercy, not sacrifice.' For I have not come to call the righteous, but sinners."

Questions:

1. What was the true food of Jesus, and what does that insinuate for our lives as his followers?
2. What did Jesus mean when he said, "I desire mercy, not sacrifice?"
3. How are we different or similar to the disciples or Pharisees?

Training

Although it might be easy to judge these two religious groups, we would be wise to first examine ourselves. What is our food? What possesses us? Is it God's mission? How do these hungry-stomached words of Jesus jive with our lives? Do we, like the Pharisees, value our religious devotion more than God's mercy reach? Compared to Jesus hangin' out with his tax collector buds, does any of our time and effort go toward those distant from God? These are penetrative questions—aren't they? Both texts highlight what happens when we, as human beings, compare ourselves closely to Christ. We encounter a scrutinizing mirror.

 **. . . for reaching out!**

Being Christians, we like his brand. But in soul-to-soul comparison, how much do we align with our Master's mind and manner? Do we look like Jesus? Most of us, if we are honest, notice a sizeable gap between our lives and his. This should stir us. We should ask, "What kind of frozen-tundra-journey do we need to make to become something 'other' than what we are right now?"

Though there is no magical wand to wave over us, we can look afresh at Jesus with a desire to follow his footsteps. Are you in? I hope so. Consider the first principle to embrace and meditate on. As a group please read it out loud:

Principle: *Being on mission is about being more like Jesus.*

Mission is first and foremost about growing into Christ-likeness. Jesus is the healthiest, most sound, rightly focused, loving person who ever walked this planet. And he was sent here on a mission to reach others for God. We could synthesize it this way: "Sound people, seek people." It was true of Jesus; it can be true of us as well. If you are spiritually healthy, you will care very much about imparting your faith. Love rightfully focuses on other's welfare; it seeks their very best.

The Bible describes Jesus in this way: "When he saw the crowds, he had compassion on them, because they were harassed and helpless, like sheep without a shepherd" (Matt 9:36). Notice how Jesus saw *life condi-*

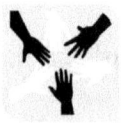 Gathering together

tion needs and *spiritual needs*. As to their life condition, they were "harassed and helpless," but he also saw their overarching need for a "Shepherd." In the same holistic way, he didn't just heal people; he came to bring them into right relationship with the Father—where all blessings flow. This, too, must be our approach. Mission will make *you* more like Jesus in compassion and spiritual influence. He seeks your emulation in both expressions.

Some have asked if pursuing relationships for the gospel's sake is disingenuous. Let's answer it. Jesus came to "seek and to save that which is lost." We know from his story that it was not always a pleasant and enjoyable undertaking with fallen human beings. Yet being fully aware of all our sinful unattractiveness, he still sought us. Did that make him, then, disingenuous? No way! With loving commitment, he embraced sinners as his friends (John 15:12–17).

Rest assured, we will cultivate *authentic friendships* where we enjoy other's company (as much as possible). No one wants to feel like someone's project—so let's not fall short here. If you are stretched relationally, allow it to shape the fullness of your character. Real love is always bigger than what we get out of it. Principally, mission parallels marriage, which requires spouses to be less selfish, or else! When you pursue his mission, it will enlarge your love and life. Guaranteed.

Contrary to it being disingenuous, evangelistic mission demonstrates love at its highest. *It makes the greatest effort for the greatest good of another human being.* It

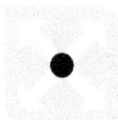   . . . **for reaching out!**

values people in the truest sense, as those made in God's image whom Christ died for. If you know the gospel, then you understand that all one's present experience and eternity are at stake! Coming to Christ will transform lives in every way with: grace, hope, power, truth, security, love, fruit, provision, peace, authenticity, community, support, salvation, etc. We earnestly want them to have all of God's infinite resources! This is why helping them to know God is so important.

In his grand design, God's knows the mission endeavor will change you, too. You may be asking, "How so?"

Your Growth Through this Series

The wise adage says, "There's the classroom and then there's the laboratory." The fact is you can only learn so much in a pew or chair! To become the person Christ meant you to be, you must *go to grow.* Let's spell out specific ways you can expect to grow in this series:

- You will grow in love.
- You will grow in sensitivity to non-believer's needs and heart dispositions.
- You will grow in compassion as you fathom other's lives without Christ.
- You will grow in service from giving of yourself.
- You will grow in authenticity and other relationship-deepening patterns.
- You will grow in spiritual influence skills.

 **Gathering together**

- You will grow in the knowledge of what Christ brings to people's lives.
- You will grow in intercessory prayer for your friends.
- You will grow in dependence upon the Holy Spirit to guide your actions and words.
- You will grow in your excitement about your role in God's mission!

Group Exercise:

Break up into threes. Each person will write out a simple one-sentence prayer for God to make their heart more like his. Mission is an inside job. It's what God has to do in us. Here are a few prayer examples for inspiration, but each person must use their own words.

> "Do in me what you need to do—so that you can do through me what you want to do."

> "Sear my heart with your love for the lost."

> "Smash this selfish stone-like heart of mine!"

> "Help me learn your manner, so I can be your messenger."

What mission prayer will you offer to God? It does not have to be eloquent, just from the heart. Go ahead and take several minutes by yourself to write something down that reflects your personal sentiment. Come back, and share what you've written with the group.

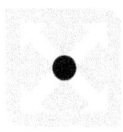 **. . . for reaching out!**

Engagement:

In preparation for what's ahead, take the time to brainstorm, as a group, ideas for an "ongoing" community project. Read the list below to get your thoughts moving on possibilities. Each community group will need to assess its localized needs and look for opportunities that lie within your neighborhood or broader region. Consider a few suggestions.

- Build a community garden
- Engage in a beautifying venture
- Provide an ongoing service
- Serve an existing compassion outreach to people marginalized in our culture
- Design a neighborhood gathering along mutual needs
- Throw a block party or barbeque
- Organize to meet needs of neighbor families
- Raise benevolence funds for a specific cause

By design, every group will determine their own project, set out the time to engage over an extended period, and invite not-yet-in-the faith neighbors to participate alongside.

 Gathering together

Important Details:

- Community groups within a particular region can combine forces. In fact, we encourage you to partner together in your outreach efforts!
- Each community group will also plan social gatherings (block party or BBQ) to invite their non-believing friends.

Next week, during the engagement time, share your ideas. It will help if one or more step up for a preparatory pre-assignment. Who is willing to get out there this week, drive through your community, and do some initial researching of pressing needs? Open your eyes to your neighborhood and area. Pray and seek God for how your group can be a blessing!

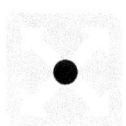 **. . . for reaching out!**

Week #2—BUILD: When Faith is Fantastic

Please read in preparation for your study:

Building homes in Mexico, a mission's team encountered an unexpected problem. Due to space constraints they had framed the roof on the road and then realized it would not make it past the entrance gate. Oops! Racking their brains, the only possible solution was to carry the roof over the roof. No kidding! It was one of the crazier ideas any of them had bought into. It took everyone, lifting and careening it over a metal gate and under a wire, fighting off neighbor dogs, jumping to the roof, carrying it across, and then scooting it into position at its final resting place. Succeeding, the group sat around exulting saying how they will never forget "the roof over the roof!"

Even greater joy must have filled four men after lugging a stretcher through a crowd, lifting it onto a roof, and then busting unabashedly through. The fantastic four's effort succeeded to position a crippled friend before Jesus. Let us take a closer look at this amazing story.

Read Passage: Mark 2:1–5

> *A few days later, when Jesus again entered Capernaum, the people heard he had come home. ²They gathered in such large numbers that there was no room left, not even outside the door, and he preached the word to them. ³Some men came, bringing to him a paralytic, carried by four of them. ⁴Since they could not get him to Jesus because of the crowd, they made an opening in the roof above Jesus and, after digging through it, lowered the mat the paralyzed man was lying on. ⁵When Jesus saw their faith, he said to the paralytic, "Son, your sins are forgiven."*

Questions:

1. What do you think was going through the minds of these men that enabled them to make such an effort?
2. Is it possible, they doubted or second-guessed the sweat-inducing endeavor for their friend? Why or why not?
3. What is it precisely that increases one's faith for reaching others?

Training

Defying our standard theological limits, Jesus sees "their faith" and says, "Son, your sins are forgiven." The principle of this text is crystal clear. Again, read the principle together out loud:

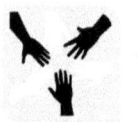 Gathering together

Principle: *My faith is directly linked to their salvation.*

Perhaps we should all complain that this principle puts *too much onus on us!* I am not responsible for someone else's faith—am I? Let's be quick to affirm that salvation comes from God. Consider, however, that if the four men in this story did not believe Jesus could heal their friend—they would not have made the effort.

As a result, their friend would not have gotten healed or saved that day. Additionally, we wouldn't have this story in our Bibles to inspire us. It was their faith that made it possible for God to touch him, and Jesus recognized this by singling them out. Look at the text again, seeing *"their faith"* he looks to the man and says, "your sins are forgiven."

This principle is challenging! Let's have it penetrate our hearts. Do we *really believe* that God can help, save, heal, transform and bless our friends? Do we believe that *Jesus* can meet their pressing needs? Mission always begins with belief. If you believe that he wills to do something miraculous, then you can summon the courage to make the monumental effort.

Fellow believers, let's talk straight! It will take a focused commitment to reach someone: *Your neighbor. Friend. Work associate. Playmate. Business connection.* If you believe that God will use you and your group, and that he can ultimately save and transform them, then your faith can be—fantastic!

Take a moment to talk honestly about your doubts. We all have them. Yet at times, doubt can be nothing

 **. . . for reaching out!**

more than a bad idea, crippling us, and undermining the work of God. Read aloud these probing questions and then interact as a group:

- Do you have any doubts regarding your personal standing with Christ to work through? (If you do, please share with your leaders/group to discuss after the session).
- What hinders your belief that God can use *you* to reach someone?
- On a scale of 1 to 10, give yourself a number on your initial faith level that the investment you and your group make with those outside the church *will actually pay off*?

Group Prayer:

Have someone pray out for the faith necessary to touch your community, and reach your friends. It is okay to pray, "Lord I believe, but help me in my unbelief." Ask God to teach you to trust him on *what to say* to your nonbelieving friends? Boldly seek God to reveal his dreams of how he wills to use your group! Before you pray, remember, who you are addressing. Paul writes, "Now to him who is able to do immeasurably more than all we ask or imagine" (Eph 3:20).

 Gathering together

Two Types of Non-Believers *You* Will Meet

1. Friends or contacts that would come to church or your group if they were invited. They are inside what I term "The Joining Circle." If you have influence, then use it to draw them in.

2. Friends or contacts that are not-yet-open to attend church or your group. They are outside the joining circle at this juncture of their journey.

Here's the billion-dollar question: Which of these types do we want to reach? The answer: both! Jesus is seeking both types, not just those who will come to us. For that to happen, a Christian must be willing to enter their world, camping out with them, so to speak. If you are willing to venture onto their turf, those outside the joining circle, in time, will come to the place of entering our world at church, on our turf!

Typically, reaching those inside the joining circle can happen collectively. By individuals building relationships and inviting them in, the church or group can eventually establish their faith. But for those outside the joining

 **. . . for reaching out!**

circle, the individual Christian that God has positioned and assigned for that relationship, will do the bulk of lifting. In fact, the individual Christian becomes their primary circle of influence. They may be the one who leads them to faith prior to their church involvement, or later amid the group time. Let's remember, we wield a mobile, unconfined gospel! Mission impels us to go!

Group Exercise:

Since the gospel flows though relationships, it links directly to your relational influence ability. Let's have the courage to ask a few questions, which reveal something of how others perceive us. Don't be afraid to sharpen each other for a noble task. Here we go. What is it like to sit inside your relational circle? In other words, when you get close with a non-believer, what will they pick up right away? Do they get anything from your persona, demeanor, attitude, words or hygiene?

Take fifteen to twenty minutes in groups of three. First, go around to affirm each person's relational qualities. What are obvious relational strengths to be maximized? Second, add your own input on how you think you could grow as an influencer. Optionally, and only if you feel comfortable, invite the others to speak into your life on how you might grow in influencing others for Christ. As examples, maybe you need to: *listen better, show love more tangibly, smile once in awhile, sustain eye-contact, learn to discuss faith, be more interested in them,*

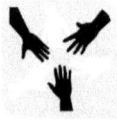 Gathering together

or suck an occasional breath mint! "As iron sharpens iron," let us sharpen one another!

Engagement:

1. Identify by name your non-believing neighbors and friends. Talk about friends you know who are outside the faith but within your relational-regional sphere. Assign a secretary to make a list. If your group has an artist, then draw or paint the hand of Jesus with its stigmata (wound), and then write their names on the canvas. Then, use the list, as an ongoing reminder to be prayerfully interceding that God would draw these precious souls. When an individual comes to faith, make a red splash over their names to commemorate that the blood of Christ now covers them!

2. Report on this past week's research regarding possible group projects. Discuss the merits of your best ideas. Which two or three are most favorable and why? Again, consider that you are doing an ongoing project and will be inviting non-believing friends participation. Next week, the group must decide on a project to pursue. Do whatever is needed this week to make that determination.

 **. . . for reaching out!**

Week #3 — BUILD: Learning Faith Formation Process

Please read in preparation for your study:

The Sawdust Festival in Laguna Beach was a browser's paradise, but nothing drew as big a crowd as the glass-blowing exhibit. The woman "gaffer" stands before a fiery furnace ironically named "the glory hole." This kiln portal provides access to the 2,300-degrees necessary to bring glass mixed with sand into a liquefied state. She dips and then retrieves the pole from the burning hot flames, spinning it to get a small ball at the end. When it is perfectly uniform she blows through the pole, which begins a bubble. She spins and shapes it on flat heat absorbing material called "the marver."

Then it goes back into the furnace to repeat the process with even larger amounts of glass. She blows it much bigger this time, constantly spinning and shaping it toward her artistic vision. Again, it goes back in the glory hole and the sequence is repeated a third time. Then she pulls out new tools to cut into the glass for a vase-like contour, still working it with even more spinning and shaping, and periodic heating with a blowtorch. Finally, she adds strips of red color. This is the intricate, timely process of turning liquid-glass into an object of beauty.

Have you ever built, formed, created or crafted something by hand? What was it? A glass vase? Clay pot? Painting? Sculpture? Go-cart? Structure? Engine? Paper airplane? Rocket? Skyscraper? Physical formation of just about anything is an art. It usually requires some type of particularized process that harnesses a number of skills. The formation of faith in the life of a non-believer is no different. It, too, is a skillful art. There is an intuitive feel involved requiring . . . sequential steps . . . specific skills . . . and an appropriate amount of time.

For this session's study, consider two very insightful paralleling passages on how Jesus engaged people in a particular pattern. The textual details, described herein, reveal a signature. Let's enter the company of his closest companions, journeying along the seaside villages of Galilee, to observe closely the Master's method. As his understudies, we can discover a guiding principle on how to relate most fruitfully.

Read Passages: Mark 7:32–34; Mark 8:22–25

> [32]There some people brought to him a man who was deaf and could hardly talk, and they begged him to place his hand on the man. [33]After he took him aside, away from the crowd, Jesus put his fingers into the man's ears. Then he spit and touched the man's tongue. [34]He looked up to heaven and

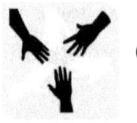 **Gathering together**

with a deep sigh said to him, "Ephphatha!" (Which means, "Be opened!").

²²They came to Bethsaida, and some people brought a blind man and begged Jesus to touch him. ²³He took the blind man by the hand and led him outside the village. When he had spit on the man's eyes and put his hands on him, Jesus asked, "Do you see anything?" ²⁴He looked up and said, "I see people; they look like trees walking around." ²⁵Once more Jesus put his hands on the man's eyes. Then his eyes were opened . . .

Questions:

1. In the first passage, how many distinct action steps are noted? What does that suggest?
2. Why do you think Jesus worked through progressions, when he could have easily healed each man immediately by the sheer power of his word?
3. How might have any of these actions inspired their faith? Which ones? Be specific.

Training

When it comes to mission, these back-to-back passages are significant because they show how Jesus engaged in a sequential pattern. Notice how intimate they are: Fingers in the ears— that means earwax; saliva on the man's tongue—it's like they kissed!

 **. . . for reaching out!**

It becomes apparent that Jesus's ultimate goal was not merely to heal, but to bring each man to faith. He could have, as with the Roman Centurion's servant, healed them from a distance. Yet true to his faith formulating pattern, Jesus instead: connected personally, held hands, walked with them for sometime, empathized with their painful predicament, touched them physically, used his actions to create anticipation, pointed to God by looking upward, prayed passionately, laid hands repetitively, and even healed. By portraying many intimate steps in a sequence, it's like Jesus is saying "Watch me; this is how it's done!"

Clearly, Jesus wants us to see disciple making in a multi-dimensional way. Like him, we are not only trying to share a message, but are initiating a spiritual journey with experiential aspects. Typically today, reaching people requires your own version of holding hands and walking alongside someone. This is usually necessary for them to see what faith does—and how it meaningfully integrates with their life. Please read the principle out loud together:

> **Principle:** *Faith formation occurs within an intimate relational process.*

According to Jesus's pattern, let's picture evangelistic engagement by the metaphor of a *lighted journey*. Your aim is to initiate a journey that will ultimately illumine a friend spiritually. Like the ancient torches that used substances like tar, animal fat, whale oil, or pine pitch to burn

 **Gathering together**

long, you seek to create a lasting, ongoing conversation. When you light a torch for your friend's path, you will find it will also brighten your own! God will teach you many things.

If we breakdown your mission adventure into critical stages it looks like this:

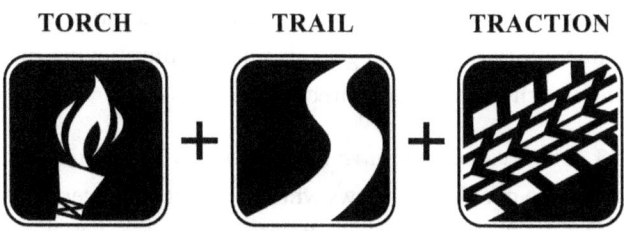

TORCH + **TRAIL** + **TRACTION**

There's the beginning stage of engaging relationally and starting a spiritual conversation (torch), a mid part of progressing down a path of exploration (trail), and a stage to gain inertia toward the faith commitment (traction). The order is important. Mix it up, or fail to pay attention to process dynamics and you can easily flub it.

In this training session, we will outline what each stage will look like. Let's begin by considering some possible scenarios that lie before you, and then we will provide helpful tips for being wise and effective. Are you ready?

Possible Scenarios: Which Applies to You?

#1 Don has a non-believing neighbor that he hardly knows. Nothing will happen spiritually, if Don does not decide to engage in a continuous manner. Don must be willing

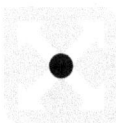 ... for reaching out!

to begin and value that relationship, and eventually get a conversation moving in a spiritual trajectory. Don must light the torch!

#2 Janie has a non-believing friend. Though Janie loves her friend, she confesses to not having made much friendship investment in some time, and has never truly gotten to the place of meaningful conversation about faith. Janie must figure out how to get this relationship moving in a new spiritually focused direction.

#3 Serenity does not have any non-believing friends. But there are people she knows who are not yet believers. She must prayerfully get herself into position relationally, where influence can develop. She must, too, light a torch!

Group Exercise:

Break into groups of three. Discuss how God has positioned you with someone outside the faith, or someone you could reach towards. Also, what could you do to create experiential elements with this person? Look at the questions below to see if any joggle your thinking.

- What would it look like to walk "hand in hand" together?
- What actions could take you to more intimate, meaningful levels?
- What experience can you lead them into that could be impactful?

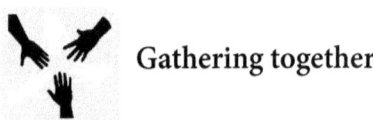 **Gathering together**

- What kind of follow up conversations would benefit your friend's journey?
- What feeling could you invoke to connect with faith?
- What picture might you paint to give perspective on faith's meaning?
- What pinpointed challenge do they need to hear from you?
- What is the next step in their progression towards God?

Journey Exercise:

With the whole group back together, take a couple minutes for each person to read the Torch, Trail and Traction Tips below. Please underline any bullets that grab your attention. Then, share together your thoughts to sharpen each other!

Torch Tips: Get the journey started! (Can you hear? "Get the party started!")

- Engage in building relationship with a specific non-believing person. The mission of reaching people never gets dynamic until it gets specific. *Stop trying to reach the world, start trying to reach someone!* God does not hold you responsible to reach the world; he wants you to reach your world. Who will you invest

 ... for reaching out!

in? You might start by getting to know your neighbor's names. Write them down and begin praying!

- Do not expect an unchurched friend to think, act, or believe like you do. Just love, accept and honor them right where they are.

- Look for ways to get together in an ongoing fashion. Coffee! Hangin' out. Fitness. Conversation. Dinner! Join a community organization. Go with them places. Invite them along!

- When the time is right (usually after some investment), ask non-threatening, open-ended (not answerable by a simple: yes or no) questions to try to understand some of their thinking about God, church and faith. "What has your experience with church been like?" Or "What is your view of God?" Or "Why do you think faith is important to some people?" "Do you think religious people are a bunch of freaks?"

- At the right moment of relational progression, connect your friend with your group to create a sense of inclusion!

Trail Tips: Walk alongside consistently.

- As you build relationship, cultivate an ongoing conversation. You can pursue specific conversational lines: (1) getting together to share life stories, (2) learning together from a spiritually related book

 Gathering together

or Bible study (3) spending time together seeking answers to their spiritual questions or objections.

- Be a safe person for them to talk with. Do not expect them to think like you do. It is absolutely okay to disagree and to have a great relationship! Sometimes, you need to wait to have deeper influencing conversations after they sense your relationship is solid and secure.

- Manage the pace of content by not overwhelming with too much too soon! Rule: The higher their attraction toward faith the more serious the conversation can go. If their interest is low—then go slow. Think of a dating relationship. Do you really want to talk about getting married on the first date? Only when it's love at first sight!

- Honor them for their qualities, ideas and contribution in the group or with a project.

- Maintain momentum by meeting regularly (weekly works best!). Let the process work for you. Do not be disheartened. *What will not happen today can happen tomorrow.* As you are praying earnestly for God's drawing, be patient in allowing the conversational seeds to take root.

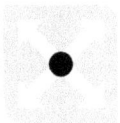 **. . . for reaching out!**

Traction Tips: Lead them into a disciples' faith.

- Address their questions. Circle back if you do not have the answers initially. Digging for answers will sharpen you and help them over barriers!
- Prepare them for faith by explaining Christian truths and the way of a disciple.
- Anticipate their coming to faith. *Be the first to believe they will believe!*
- Invite them to church and your group's gatherings. If they are moving forward, encourage them to be seeking God experientially through prayer.
- The time will come, usually later in the journey, when it can be potent to ask *where they are* regarding following Christ. Note: Session 7 will give you several ways to lead them to faith.

All three stages are critical. Like the glassblower who must respect the stages of a process, you can lose a nonbeliever if you do not pay attention and work at reaching them.

Engagement:

1. This week the group will decide on a specific community project. Following the group decision, you must designate a project leader. The project leader's role is to oversee the organizational details, assemble a team, and mobilize the members.

 **Gathering together**

2. Take time to add any names of non-believers within your sphere, and pray specifically for your list. This week, we are asking you to figure a way to engage them relationally. How can you act to position or reposition yourself for an ongoing conversation? What can you do initially to light a torch for a journey? Come prepared next week to share about the doors that God is opening!

 ... for reaching out!

Week #4—BENEFIT: Getting Real For the Gospel

Please read in preparation for your study:

Why don't we just admit that talking with non-believers about faith can be awkward, intimidating and even scary? For most it's not as frightening as public speaking, but some think—it's close! Go around the circle and pick a number on a scale of 1 to 10 to communicate your comfort level in sharing your faith with others.

>1—I am intimidated and terrified!
>
>5—I feel challenged, but I have done it some, and am progressing.
>
>10—I feel comfortable and invigorated by sharing my faith.

Though different comfort levels exist, the next sessions will sharpen everyone to be more natural, less threatening, and effective! We will focus on displaying the *benefits* of faith. As you continually build relationship, the time will come when you will want to deepen that relationship and communicate something spiritually substantive. This, however, is not always simple to do. That's why you need to learn some new skills!

Let's first reframe the way we approach evangelism. Instead of thinking that you have to tell the whole Christian story (which can be too much too soon and awkward), we want you, rather, to think in terms of creating a "faith-glimpse." Your aim is to help your friend see something of faith's relevancy to their life.

Two practices offer this kind of window in a way that can be natural for you in conversations. We call them: The *Disclosure* and *Description Windows*. In other words, you can provide a glimpse to the benefit of knowing Christ by disclosing your life, or by describing faith's appeal.

In today's session we will focus exclusively on the *Disclosure Window*. Next week we'll cover *Description*. As you might have already guessed, this week is about getting real for the gospel. You can provide a non-believing friend a glimpse of faith's meaning when you disclose your own story, with its assorted swashes of darkness, as a backdrop to God's light! Being authentic, a beloved trademark value of the Bible is also a powerful means of sharing the gospel! This is especially true in our postmodern time. Please take a look at the words of Jesus, and also a verse from the Apostle Paul.

Read Passages: Mark 4:21; 2 Cor 4:7

> *²¹"Do you bring in a lamp to put it under a bowl or a bed? Instead, don't you put it on its stand? For whatever is hidden is meant to be disclosed, and whatever is concealed is meant to be brought out into the open."*

 **Gathering together**

Questions:

1. From the lamp illustration, what happens when we hide or conceal our lives from non-believers?

   ⁷But we have this treasure in jars of clay to show that this all-surpassing power is from God and not from us.

2. What is the meaning of the "jars of clay" metaphor?

3. How can non-believing people see that the power is from God and not us? In other words, why would they not just say that you're a goodie-goodie religious freak?

Training

Numerous benefits arise from getting real with your non-believing friends. Please consider the following dynamics that occur when you open up and disclose something honest, personal, or vulnerable:

- It deepens the relational bond: *Perhaps drawing them to share as well.*
- It reveals Christianity's true picture: *Christ's power in our weakness.*
- It shapes the non-believer toward humility: *They, too, have sins to own!*
- It sheds the hypocrite label: *We're not pretending to be something we're not!*

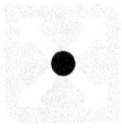 **. . . for reaching out!**

- It shows a picture of how Christ helps us: *They need his help too!*

Of course, disclosure has its appropriate moments and measures. We are not always disclosing (that could come across as overly needy, or that we are dumping our burdens on them). Nor do we want to overwhelm them with too much disclosure in a first time chat! Yet in the right context of a developing relationship, there will be times when utilizing this window can deepen their connection with you and open their eyes to faith. Read together out loud this session's principle:

> **Principle:** *They may never see Christ's light if they don't see my darkness.*

Below are four ways to utilize the disclosure window. After the definitions, you are going to have the opportunity to practice disclosing with one another. So pay attention! You should be able to see yourself in all four categories.

Sin

This delves into our biblically described fallen condition. Because our sin nature is not eradicated, we must manage our sin condition, and yield to Christ for heavenly help. Where are you most prone to be vulnerable? Pride? Anger? Lust? Fear? Gluttony? Laziness? Selfishness? Deceit? Greed? Envy? What is it? Where do you need Christ to forgive, restore, and empower you? Ironically,

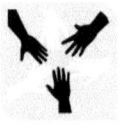 **Gathering together**

sharing your human predicament might be one of the most powerful ways to share Christ!

Struggle

Not necessarily sin, this category relates to ongoing life issues and difficulties: crazy circumstances, health issues, trials, etc. This type of disclosure reveals the challenges we are facing right now. As Christians, life is not problem-free, but we walk through life's difficulties with the Lord.

Striving

Here we recognize what we have not yet been able to achieve. Like keeping a diet, developing new habits, getting over a hurt, loving the hard to love, letting go, forgiving someone, reaching a spiritual goal, or growing a group or ministry. This type of disclosure showcases our limitations. It reveals in a deep way our need for God's grace and supernatural intervention.

Story

Your story involves the conflicts God has placed before you. What have you had to overcome or are in need of overcoming right now? Like Paul's hindering thorn, and Peter's shameful denials, these obstacles deepen dependence and spiritual character. They force us to dig down with God to find his strength to rise above. Story often displays God's redemption of our brokenness.

 **... for reaching out!**

Please note that non-believers face the same challenges as you! In this way, we are no different. Our difference is that we have Christ, and his grace and power. When we share authentically about ourselves, we also share authentically about Jesus. Outside of sharing your need for Christ, they may never take-in what they truly needed to hear. As the Apostle John wrote, "The light shines in the darkness!"

For your personal study, observe the four disclosures modeled by Paul:

The Apostle Paul's Disclosure Window		
SIN	*Sin-Nature Vulnerabilities*	Rom 7:14–25
STRUGGLE	*Life Difficulties*	2 Cor 1:8–9; 1 Cor 2:3; 2 Cor 2:4
STRIVING	*Limitations to Achieving*	1 Thess 2:17–18; 2 Cor 1:23–2:2
STORY	*Overcoming Obstacles*	2 Cor 12:6–10; 2 Cor 6:3–10

Group Exercise:

Break into groups of three. We are going to give you twenty-minutes to disclose something of your life. Use one of the four disclosure angles. When you do so, think

Gathering together

of how you would share in a way that would help a non-believing person get to know you more deeply and also see something about your faith. In other words, your aim is to share authentically, but also in a way that reveals how Christ helps you.

Engagement:

1. Delegate out project preparation tasks.
2. In a faith formation gesture, step out to show love this week to your unchurched neighbors and friends through an act of kindness. Take a moment together to brainstorm ideas (a note, call, gift, invite, apology, etc.). Remember, it doesn't have to be big to be super-impactful!
3. In the days/weeks ahead, look for the opportunity to share something "real" with a non-believing friend.

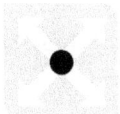 **. . . for reaching out!**

Week #5 —BENEFIT: The Gospel and Its Key

Please read in preparation for your study:

If, by chance, your non-believing friend is hungrily chompin' at the bit to learn Christian truths, then your role is to explain Christ's intervention in this world on their behalf, and to lead them to trust Jesus for forgiveness and salvation. Let's not ever make it more difficult than it is. Oftentimes, however, that is not the case with our outside-the-faith friends. This leaves us wondering how to talk with them about spiritual things in a way that is not awkward or ineffectual.

This session provides training on the second glimpse to faith: *The Description Window*. Describing faith can help non-believers see its relevancy. It is also a great way to begin a spiritual conversation. Jesus provides a potent example of how to do this in John chapter 4 in his encounter with a Samaritan woman. Please read this exchange with a fresh, scrutinizing eye.

Passage: John 4:10–15

> [10] Jesus answered her, "If you knew the gift of God and who it is that asks you for a drink, you would have asked him and he would have given you living water."
>
> [11] "Sir," the woman said, "you have nothing to draw with and the well is deep. Where can you get this living water? [12] Are you greater than our father Jacob, who gave us the well and drank from it himself, as did also his sons and his livestock?"
>
> [13] Jesus answered, "Everyone who drinks this water will be thirsty again, [14] but whoever drinks the water I give them will never thirst. Indeed, the water I give them will become in them a spring of water welling up to eternal life."
>
> [15] The woman said to him, "Sir, give me this water so that I won't get thirsty and have to keep coming here to draw water."

Questions:

1. Is there symbolism between the woman's life and the well? How so?

2. Besides her physical thirst, why do you think Jesus chose the metaphor "living water?"

3. From the dialogue, do you see anything indicating that she suspected Jesus meant something more than H20?

 Gathering together

Training

This Samaritan woman, (referred to as Samantha) is carrying out the routine task of drawing water when Jesus engages her about "living water" that would well up within her. With those few descriptive words her mind is transported to an entirely new picture of what her life could be. Behold the power of words! You should recognize that, like Jesus, you can paint a picture for your non-believing friends. If Jesus had said nothing, Samantha would not have realized who it was who graced her presence, and what he could offer.

Notice Jesus does not tell her what she needs; he draws according to her need. She had repeatedly traveled out to the well for water, and in a deeper sense had sought to fill her soul with numerous relationships (five marriages and a live-in boyfriend!) Samantha was searching for something only Jesus could provide: a perpetual infilling to quench her thirsting soul. He describes it with the metaphor: "living water." When she heard those prescriptive words—it drew her—she wanted it! From this passage, we find a very potent faith-sharing principle. As a group please read it aloud:

> **Principle:** *Assess their needs deeply to describe the gospel powerfully.*

By learning to describe faith according to your friend's particular needs, your words, too, can have pinpointed power! Observe what is involved with this win-

   **. . . for reaching out!**

dow. Like Jesus, you have to first read your friend's needs. Then you can share something about faith that has resonating appeal. This window begins a conversation about how faith intersects personally, connecting faith to their life situation (grey area of graph).

It is not a direct conversation about the cross, but rather a discussion about its implicational meaning. I have termed this approach: "The gospel key," because these types of conversations, like the one Jesus had with Samantha, can turn the pin and tumblers inside a person's heart! This is a higher-level sharing technique that Jesus used; and one that we can learn to utilize as well.

Consider the sequence of the description window:

 Gathering together

It begins with listening. Initially, you will most likely not know your friend's key. Effective evangelism starts by probingly discerning *where they are at* right now. In the relational context, you will have to ask questions to draw out information about your unsaved friend to gain insight about their needs, drives, and dreams. For some, this is easy, because they talk openly about their life. For others, however, you will have to work at getting them to open up and reveal more. By getting to know them personally, you are listening for how the gospel would resonate in a personally prescriptive way. Consider a couple real life examples:

Janel's Story: Kayla, active in the military, prepared to ship off on her new assignment. As she disclosed anxieties on what awaited her, Janel saw how devoid she was of anything solid, unchanging, and anchoring. This insight led to a conversation about faith. Janel jumped in and described what it meant to know Christ; he was the steady, guiding, ever-present compass and companion she lacked. Kayla suddenly saw faith in a new light. Pursuing her interest, Janel then uncovered her cousin's "having to be perfect" view of Christianity. When she explained that the very reason we need Christ is because we're all flawed, Janel led Kayla into the faith!

 **. . . for reaching out!**

Sean's Story: Sean is a Christian electrician. Tom is an atheist-agnostic electrician, who works side-by-side with Sean. During their labor, Sean discloses a number of personal issues. He and his wife had recently separated. By disclosing, Tom learned of Sean's beliefs as he is seeking God to help his marriage. Reciprocating, Tom shared some of his challenges as well.

Listening intently, Sean noticed a theme. Tom has major problems with stress. He especially noted when Tom said, "I feel like I carry the weight of the world on my shoulders." Being trained in this skill, Sean recognized a key. He then initiated conversation about Jesus's words, "Come to me, all who are weary and burdened, and I will give you rest" (Matt 11:28). This begins a dialogue. Not surprisingly, Tom responded engagingly. A week following, Sean discovered that Tom went to buy a Bible. Three weeks later, he began attending church. Months later, he came to faith!

Group Exercise:

Break into threes for a twenty-minute exercise. First, to the best of your ability describe what drew you into the faith. What was your motivation to follow Christ? According to your story, what appealed at a heart level?

Second, discuss what you think the key message *might be* for a non-believing friend. Granted, you may not know what would draw them. But guess? Put yourself into their shoes. Study them. Hack into their mainframe

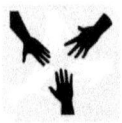 Gathering together

to get a true look at what's really going on. What would be the messaging key to move the pin and tumblers inside their heart?

Training: The Drawing Process

Observe carefully how Jesus used the description window with Samantha. He said, "If you knew the gift of God and who it is that asks you for a drink, you would have asked him and he would have given you living water." From this verse comes a three step drawing process:

1. Discover their key

2. Describe their benefit

3. Direct their response

Like Samantha, non-believers don't know what the gift of God is. Jesus understood that he would have to help her see what a relationship with him would mean. This applies to all our redemptive relationships as well. We are the ones who must assess the spiritual remedy to their life's pursuits, which will guide what we share.

Pointing to the significance of *who he is*, we distinguish his offering. She could get water from many places, but only Jesus offered "living water." In our communication, we focus on a spiritual benefit of knowing God. Just as Jesus described the benefit vividly through the term "living water," we, too, must create a descriptive picture. Not that it has to be a metaphor, but the idea is to describe what it would mean for them to have a relationship with

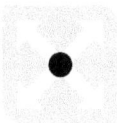 **. . . for reaching out!**

Christ. When communicating, like an artist you paint a picture of a preferred life, a window to what they could experience.

Finally, within this descriptive offer, Jesus extends an invitation for her to seek him for the gift: *"you would of asked him and he would have given you living water."* To do this, you simply answer the question of the person's coming to faith. If my friend became a Christian, I see this happening—_____ (fill in the blank). That, by the way, is exactly how you convey it: "If you were to become a Christian, I see this happening in your life."

Sometimes it helps to envision what their life would look like a couple years down the road, if they turned to Christ. Project outward to garner the insight. What difference would Jesus make? When you work this drawing process all the way to providing a compelling picture, you will be amazed at how God will use your words!

Group Role-Play Exercise:

Pick out one of the human need categories listed below that relates to someone you know. As a group, interpret descriptively what Christ could offer.

• Abuse • Marriage breakdown • Low self worth • Health issues • Boredom • Addiction • Driven lifestyle • New parent • Spiritually empty • Job/Financial difficulties • World Changer • Emotional loss • Lonely • Broken • Anxious • Legal troubles • Adultery • Conflict problems

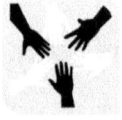 **Gathering together**

Observe several examples of how to communicate the key:

- Anna (abandoned by her spouse) . . . "When you become a Christian, you will experience how God will always be there for you—it will give you a deep sense of security knowing he will never leave you. Earthly relationships will fail us, but God never will. You can learn to depend on him as he walks with you into your future."

- Les (broken by his mistakes) . . . "God is able to redeem your failures. This is what God does. He takes all the pieces and works them together for good. If you follow him, you will be amazed to see how he can redeem your life."

- Jackson (success-driven) . . . "Your ambitions could be fulfilled in bigger ways than you could ever imagine. By serving Christ, you will discover a level of significance that is far greater than anything this world offers. Worldly success is temporary and empty; his reward lasts and fulfills."

- Alex (marital troubles) . . . "If you follow Christ you will discover what Christ can do for your marriage. He can begin delivering you from your selfishness that's at the root of all problems. The only way, though, is putting him first. When you do, he will heal your marriage by changing you from the inside out."

 **. . . for reaching out!**

- Jenny (self-esteem deficient) . . . "God can help you come into a full realization of just how important and precious you are. He made you for a relationship with him. You are the highest of his creation but he wants you to know that in a profoundly personal way. If you decide to follow Christ you will experience forgiveness and the touch of his loving presence within you."

- Frank (anxiety bound) . . . "Through a relationship with God you could replace the worry you feel right now with his peace. It all comes through having that trusting relationship with him. If you come to know Christ, you will be blown away by his ability to personally care and provide for you."

Communication Tips

Once you have discovered their key and interpreted what the message would be for them, then, you must communicate it. Sometimes this happens spontaneously in the conversational interchange. But there are other times when, like a poker player with a loaded hand, you will want to wait for the right intimate moment. Pull them aside, like Jesus did, and then communicate your idea about what their life could be. This can be powerful!

Sometimes, people can come to faith rather quickly! Usually it begins a dialogue about how faith will bless their life. By providing a descriptive picture, you are giving them a vision they could not project themselves. This creates a drawing effect. From there we can eventually

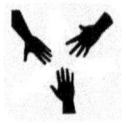 **Gathering together**

lead them into a greater discussion about the cross, and coming to know Jesus.

In review, you have learned two skills, the *Disclosure* and *Description Windows*, which can help you to seed the gospel into people's lives. Practice them! Don't be afraid to dive in! Seeding the idea of faith in a relevant way is often a million times more effective than proclaiming what they already know about Jesus. As your words germinate into piqued receptivity, trust God to bring forth his fruit!

One more thing. You are learning messaging skills that fit within the broader holistic picture of connecting and showing love to people outside the church. God will use your life, deeds and words to reach people. Persevere. Have faith and the new disciples will follow!

Engagement:

(1) Group Sharing:

What is God doing in your relationships? What can we be praying for? Do any of you see "keys" in your friend's lives that you can share with the group? If so, share about what you see and then pray for God to work through you.

(2) Assignment:

Talk about your group's project and other outreach related activities. Recall, each community group needs to plan social events as well. Those gatherings will provide impetus for relational development and influence.

 **... for reaching out!**

Week #6—BARRIERS: Discerning Belief Barriers

Please read in preparation for your study:

A married woman seeks help from her block to sexual intimacy. She had watched her father sexually abuse her sister, and though she did not recollect much, this memory led her to shut down physically. The counselor, having exhausted his efforts, did not know what else to do, so he sought help from above, saying, "God, I invite you to minister to her."

She sits bowed for a time, and then opens her eyes and says, "I was thinking about my father, and the thought came to me of how wounded of a person he must have been to do something like that." God had met her, and suddenly she was able to have compassion on him.

Afterwards, she found herself able to re-engage sexually with her husband. The counselor followed up later by asking, "Would you like to know the person who healed you?" He went on to lead her to faith. According to Dr. Dave Ferreira, there is a particular order involved. He explained, "In the counseling realm, the heart is healed before the head."

When we engage with non-believers there will be times when we will find ourselves wondering where the block lies. Is it the head or the heart? What is hindering their progression to faith? It is fascinating to ask this question in view of how Jesus responded to people in the Bible.

For instance, consider his encounters with two polar opposites in chapters 3 and 4 of John: a high-standing, moralistic Pharisee, and a common un-reputable Samaritan woman. Notice the disparateness. Each of these individuals had different starting points: ethnicities, religious backgrounds, viewpoints and lifestyles. How odd if Jesus had given them the same message. How dishonoring to their personhoods! Of course he did not!

The fact is Jesus did not make the same presentation to anyone. His exchanges with people were unique and dynamic. Part of what he does, which we can learn to do also, is that he discerns the storyline of each individual.

Biblical Study:

In this week's session, we are going to shake up our study. Instead of looking primarily to a text, we will draw on the existing Bible knowledge of the group. Many of you are familiar with the biblical characters and their stories listed below. Off the top of your heads, where did the barrier lie? In general terms, was it the head or the heart? If you need some clues, we have added key verses under the

 **Gathering together**

person. Think deeply, and then give it your best educated guess!

Take a moment to circle (on the right) where the block lies for each character:

- Nicodemus (Nick) .... head / heart

    ³Jesus replied, "Very truly I tell you, no one can see the kingdom of God unless they are born again." . . . ⁹"How can this be?" Nicodemus asked. ¹⁰"You are Israel's teacher," said Jesus, "and do you not understand these things?" (John 3:3, 9–10).

- The Samaritan Woman (Samantha) ..... head / heart

    ¹³Jesus answered, "Everyone who drinks this water will be thirsty again, ¹⁴but whoever drinks the water I give him will never thirst. Indeed, the water I give him will become in him a spring of water welling up to eternal life" (John 4:13-14).

- The Wealthy Ruler (Richie).................... head / heart

    ²⁰"Teacher," he declared, "all these (God's commandments) I have kept since I was a boy." ²¹Jesus looked at him and loved him. "One thing you lack," he said. "Go, sell everything you have and give to the poor, and you will have treasure in heaven. Then come, follow me" (Mark 10:20-21).

Group interaction:

Now take a few minutes to discuss the rationale behind your choices.

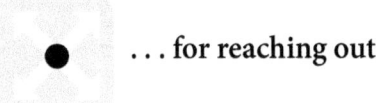 **. . . for reaching out!**

Training

Without going into all the detail of these unique conversations, we can see how Jesus assessed their real issues. For someone, like Nicodemus, the tension in the dialogue is all about understanding (the head). Nick needed to face the shocking truth that all his religiosity—meant nothing! He needed to be born anew; life comes from God's Spirit! With others, like Samantha, however, Jesus speaks to her deep soul needs (the heart), at least initially. When it gets a bit personal, five husbands and a live-in boyfriend, she resorts to more heady theological questions about worship.

Similarly, both head and heart dimensions are also evident in Jesus's interaction with the rich young ruler. Delusional, Richie thinks he's righteously good (head issue), and has wrapped his life around his wealth at idolatrous levels (heart issue). Jesus's invitation to give everything away and follow him, seeks to surgically release him from the bondage! When we look closely at these encounters, the conversation stems from the person's starting point. Sometimes it goes from the head to heart, and from heart to head. This pattern will be typical in your evangelistic dialogues.

While engaging relationally, you will find yourself pondering where the greater block lies with your friend. Which barrier, head or heart, will they need to breakthrough? This session's faith-sharing principle will help you to discern and focus. As a unified group, declare the principle out loud:

 **Gathering together**

Principle: *Reading what they need
tells me how to proceed.*

To apply this principle, you must get in-tune with your friend's backstory. Becoming adept at reading their journey is tricky at times. To sharpen your discernment skills, contemplate this real life scenario.

"We don't do the church thing in our family" was the rather curt, walk-off response from Liz to her friend Anne. How do you respond when a non-believing friend shuts down an attempt to discuss faith? Ever been there? Do we put our tail between our legs? Should we just let it go, and make a mental note to never bring it up again? Most of us have had these moments. Let's steal a page from Jesus!

First, you can practice what Jesus modeled in his pattern of circling back and finding people (John 5:12; John 9:35). Liz's response is not an end, but can be a beginning to a rich, meaningful conversation. In faith sharing, establishing an ongoing dialogue is the goal. You must, like Jesus, circle back and then draw out. Your aim, as a caring friend, would be to find out what is going on inside Liz.

As we have noted, evangelism begins with their starting point. Typically, we don't know where that is until they express it. So, as you reconnect enjoying time together, when the moment is right, you circle back saying, "The other day, Liz, when you expressed that your family did not engage with church, I didn't understand what you meant. As your friend (who values knowing you), could you explain that to me?"

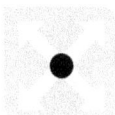 **. . . for reaching out!**

If asked in a loving sensitive tone, Liz will most likely open to share something. If she does not, that may indicate wounding. If Anne discerns a strong reaction, she will want to draw out the pain by encouraging Liz to talk so healing can begin. Like the pattern in counseling, sometimes we work through healing at the initial stage of the evangelistic process. The structure looks like this: Ask a question. Listen. Then ask a follow-up question to get more clarity, or to draw out what is undergirding their response. "What do you mean?" "Why do you feel that way?" "Can you explain so I can understand you more?"

If Anne can draw out the true thoughts and feelings from Liz, then she would know where the conversation could develop meaningfully. The only thing that is clear about Liz's initial statement is its ambiguity.

Her family's "not attending" could mean a number of things such as: (1) I grew up in a non-Christian home and church was never part of our lives, (2) I had a bad experience when a Christian I didn't even know attacked my beliefs, so I made it a rule to not ever talk about religion with anyone again, (3) When my dad died of cancer, and I watched my mom suffer, it made me angry at God. Consider the disparity of sentiment behind these three very common responses. At this juncture, however, Anne truly does not know what is happening inside her friend.

Therefore, she must first draw out her heart. This is the only way for Anne to see clearly what is needed for her friend's progression. When Liz shares her true thoughts, Anne will be able to process an appropriate course of

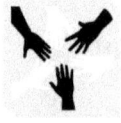 **Gathering together**

conversation. Sometimes we respond right then—sometimes later. Each example noted above requires a distinct direction.

Group Interaction:

For your skill development, how would you reply to any one of the three options: (1) We never attended, (2) Don't talk about religion, (3) Angry at God. Break into groups of three and take fifteen-minutes to discuss how you might best respond.

Training Continued . . .

Let's assume Liz's response is the simpler number one. Anne, now knowing what Liz's words meant, could respond saying something like this,

> "Liz, I know the faith subject is not always easy to discuss, but I believe it can be so meaningful with a friend. There was a time in my life when I didn't want to talk about spiritual topics either, but I was so glad when I did. I'd be honored to have that discussion with you. It can be so enriching. Rest assured, I want you to know that you don't need to do anything and you don't ever have to come to my church. We could just meet to talk."

If her response were number 2, where she had a bad experience with a Christian or the church, you would want to apologize for those actions. We should be deeply broken

   . . . **for reaching out!**

and contrite over what our group has done. Do all that you can to provide a countering image of what it truly means to be a Christian. This can bring needed healing.

To help you in assessing barriers and what it will take to reach your non-believing friend, please observe carefully the following grid:

TYPE OF NON-BELIEVER	WILL COME TO CHRIST IF...
HEAR	*The gospel is explained with clarity.*
HURDLE	*They are helped over 1 or 2 of their question hang ups.*
HAMMER	*An entirely new Christian worldview is built for them (atheists, skeptics, other faiths).*
HURTING	*They find love being held, helped & healed in Christ & his church.*

At the head level, some simply need an explanation. If you sit down and interact with this person and provide clarity about the "good news" message, they will come to faith. With others, however, a serious question or two must get resolved. Paul called these Satanic strongholds "pretensions" that have been set up against the knowledge of God (2 Cor 10:4–5). When you help them get past the hurdle they will be freed to believe.

Still others, such as skeptics and those from other religions, will need something far more substantial. Essentially, they need someone to help them build a new

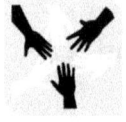 Gathering together

worldview (In my book, *Soul Whisperer*, I show how to reach these more difficult types).

Yet at the heart level, many merely need to be loved. They will respond if they are embraced, included, served, and maybe even healed before they come to Christ. The overarching question before you is: What is in the way of your friend coming to Jesus? What do they truly need? Do you know?

Here is one more question that we must ask. Are we the barrier? Do they see in us the kind of quality that draws them to our faith? Jesus treated sinners with incredible grace, honor and dignity. What about us? Do they feel safe in our presence to talk openly? Do they see how much we respect their thoughts and contributions? Do they sense in us the kind of love that seeks their well-being? Again, your character plays a big part in the mission equation. If there's something to own—then own it. You will have taken a step to being more like Jesus!

Group Exercise:

Break into threes. Share about the non-believing friend you are reaching towards. Where have conversations gone thus far? What do you know about them and their starting point? In other words, where are they on their spiritual search? Have they revealed anything that places them in one of the four categories of this chart? Go!

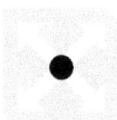 **. . . for reaching out!**

Engagement:

(1) Group Sharing:

- Small/Community Group leaders and the group itself can provide insightful input on questions your friends have. Lean on each other! Do you need help with any specific queries that have come your way?

- Report on your relationships with non-believing friends. Have any of you had opportunities to utilize the *Disclosure or Description Windows*? Remember, this series is not just about learning principles; it's about putting those principles into practice. That is when God will sharpen you most!

(2) Assignments:

- Begin your community project. Or get ready to throw a block party!

- Discuss how you plan to invite your neighbors and friends to participate with the project. Brainstorm ideas, if necessary.

 **Gathering together**

Week #7—BELIEVE / BELONG: Coming Home to Jesus

Please read in preparation for your study:

A certain father, on a Saturday morning, gathers his twelve-year old son for an important refurbishing job. The metal chairs need to get painted for the upcoming party. Laying down plastic, he assembles the supplies. As he begins to explain the task at hand, an interrupting phone call whisks dad away.

Waiting, the boy thinks to himself, "I am going to please my dad by painting one of the chairs before he gets back." Having used a spray can before, he picks up the can, shakes it some, and then goes at it. After a couple minutes of spraying, he notices something he did not anticipate. The paint is dripping. Profusely! Stopping to look closer, and feeling panicky, the young boy assumes the paint must not be working.

Returning, his father sees what is happening, and takes a moment to share his wisdom: "Son, with slick, hardened, metal surfaces, you have to scratch the exterior first to get the paint to stick. Your preparation is key.

Without ample attention given to roughing the surface, with either sandpaper or wire-brush, the desired result of getting the paint to stick—will not be achievable. Spray away all you want, without the grooves, there's nothing to hold the paint."

That day, the son learned an important lesson from his father. In this session, you will learn what your heavenly Father has to say about faith's sticking points. How do you get faith to root solidly in your friend's heart? Granted, the Holy Spirit must do his work! Yet, as influencers, how do we help them to embrace Jesus in a transformational way—so that they get established and empowered? These are worthy questions. The following text introduces this pivot-producing activity.

Read Passage: Acts 8:26–36, 38

> [26]Now an angel of the Lord said to Philip, "Go south to the road—the desert road—that goes down from Jerusalem to Gaza." [27]So he started out, and on his way he met an Ethiopian eunuch, an important official in charge of all the treasury of the Kandake (which means "queen of the Ethiopians"). This man had gone to Jerusalem to worship, [28]and on his way home was sitting in his chariot reading the Book of Isaiah the prophet. [29]The Spirit told Philip, "Go to that chariot and stay near it."
>
> [30]Then Philip ran up to the chariot and heard the man reading Isaiah the prophet. "Do you understand what you are reading?" Philip asked.

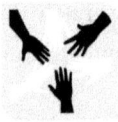 **Gathering together**

³¹"How can I," he said, "unless someone explains it to me?" So he invited Philip to come up and sit with him.

³²This is the passage of Scripture the eunuch was reading: "He was led like a sheep to the slaughter, and as a lamb before its shearer is silent, so he did not open his mouth. ³³In his humiliation he was deprived of justice. Who can speak of his descendants? For his life was taken from the earth."

³⁴The eunuch asked Philip, "Tell me, please, who is the prophet talking about, himself or someone else?" ³⁵Then Philip began with that very passage of Scripture and told him the good news about Jesus. ³⁶As they traveled along the road, they came to some water and the eunuch said, "Look, here is water. What can stand in the way of my being baptized?" ³⁸And he gave orders to stop the chariot. Then both Philip and the eunuch went down into the water and Philip baptized him.

Questions:

1. Who was this Ethiopian eunuch, and what hindered his coming to Jesus?

2. What did Philip do to foster his faith?

3. How would you compare the heart readiness of the eunuch to the heart condition of your friend or neighbor? What does that tell you?

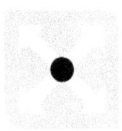   . . . **for reaching out!**

Training

Notice how several things had to occur for Philip to reach him. The Ethiopian eunuch, unlike many non-believers today, had a spiritual foundation already, evidenced by his pilgrimage to Jerusalem. Yet, as we see in the story, he was unable to realize salvation. Philip obediently came alongside, filled in the missing data, which enabled his response.

This lesson may be one of the most important training concepts. Why are we reaching so few? The human mind and heart must be amply prepared to receive and hold the divine words. This is how you reach your friends! If you go about Jesus's faith formation process, you can lovingly move your friends into responsiveness. As a group, read this session's principle together out loud:

> **Principle:** *Saving faith is the result of properly prepared hearts.*

Just like the Ethiopian eunuch, who needed assistance, every person has certain progressions they must pass through. A spiritual commitment to God is a big deal! It's like getting hitched. Would you go up to someone you just met and say, "Let's get married?" We laugh, because we know the person is not even remotely prepared for that kind of commitment. There are vital progressions that must take place first—it's called dating!

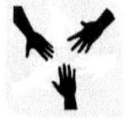 Gathering together

Group Interactive:

Go around the circle in your group, if currently in a dating relationship or married, when did you first talk about marriage? First date? Creepy! First month? (still creepy). First year? Second year and beyond? Go for it.

Training Continued . . .

The point of the exercise is to realize there is a proper progression that we must honor. Courting the non-believer is similar, and sometimes even more complex. If we see the progressions that every non-believer must go through, then we can anticipate the grooves needed to make a response possible. And we can proceed at an appropriate pace.

Take a moment to study the following graph on the four steps to faith, which offers insight on how to reach your not-yet-believing friends. Pay attention to the relationship between "THE HANG UP" and the "HELP WITH" columns.

STEPS	"THE HANG UP"	HELP WITH...
1. Open to	Interest	Asking
2. Able to	Reason	Answers
3. Want to	Motivation	Appeal
4. Choose to	Response	Application

 . . . for reaching out!

From the non-believer's starting point, you can chart the journey through these steps. Like a stairway to heaven, they move progressively upward. When seeking to reach outside-the-faith friends, it's never just about proclaiming a message, but about bringing them into: sufficient interest (open to), discernment of truth (able to), inner desire to follow (want to), and whole-hearted spiritual commitment (choose to). Every one of these movements is monumentally significant in the process.

As we see from Scripture, Jesus had penetrating insight on people's paths. Discerning their beginning point and the progressions in their journey is not unspiritual, nor does it discredit the supernatural work of God; to the contrary, we are going deep within hearts to allow the work of the Spirit—that is often when God does his wonders!

Look at each progression broken down and think about your non-believing friend or friends. Where are they in their journey? How can you come alongside, like Philip, to help them forward?

Group Exercise:

In groups of three, read silently the four actions below and discuss where you think you need to concentrate with a particular friend.

Asking:

Here, you inquire about their spiritual journey and their thoughts about faith and God. "Have you ever fathomed

 **Gathering together**

how much God cares for you personally?" "Do you ever think that going deeper with faith would benefit your life?" "Could you ever imagine yourself becoming a Christian?" *Plant seeds of interest!* Don't be shy about sharing that God loves them, and desires through a relationship with him to bless their lives beyond their wildest dreams. Ask if they would be willing to learn more with you. Drawing their initial interest to explore—is the first step on their journey to faith!

Answers:

Their questions are super-important! We can help them by discovering reasonable answers to their queries or objections. Don't be intimidated if you don't know an answer immediately. Be honest. Admit you don't know how to best reply, but then offer to do some research and circle back with them that week. In this way, their questions can launch a meaningful dialogue! *Just make sure you don't win the point, and lose the person.* Offer your thoughts, and respect theirs, even if you disagree. For many, they will need to satisfy their mental reservations before they come to faith.

Appeal:

Describe the Christian faith in a way that highlights its personal appeal. No one is devoid of self-interest. People will not follow until they see what faith will do for their life. Utilize the "windows" of disclosure and description to showcase Christianity's life-giving relevancy!

 **. . . for reaching out!**

Application:

Help them respond to Jesus through trusting Christ for salvation, committing to follow his way, getting baptized, and coming to your group and church.

In summary, our role is to help them work through the progressions to eventually respond to Jesus. Sometimes that journey happens organically as we engage with them relationally, share life and include them in our group. As they belong, the environment fills in pieces and draws them to believe! Other times, we play a very intentional role in guiding them through from one place to the other. We must, therefore, directly lead them through each step to God!

Three key preparation questions:

1. Are they comfortable with the Christian beliefs?
2. Are they comfortable with the commitment to follow Jesus?
3. Are they comfortably integrating into your group or church?

Ways to Lead People to Faith

- *Baptism:*

This will be one of the primary ways the Community Groups draw people to faith. Baptisms can occur in home

 **Gathering together**

or community pools, and at your church site. Within the group or individual conversations, invite them to put their faith in Jesus and be baptized. Take your time to explain what it means. Preparation of the heart is key.

When we inform them of the baptism, we need to be clear in calling them to follow Christ wholeheartedly. There is no magic in the waters! God looks for each individual to place their faith in what Jesus has done for them on the cross, and to repent (turn from sin to follow Jesus). We want them truly saved, not just wet!

• *Group Communion:*

Though atypical, you could use the communion event (a remembrance of Christ's sacrifice on our behalf) as a call to the faith response, but only if you have properly prepared your non-believing friends. Otherwise, they are just going through the motions, and it might even confuse them.

Yet communion could be the vehicle for saving faith, if an individual or the facilitating leader communicates that taking communion is signifying their choice to receive Christ's death on their behalf and to become his disciple. If they are not ready for that commitment, they should not participate, but only observe. If the group facilitator has done the verbal explanation to make it their commitment, communion could initiate salvation.

   ... for reaching out!

- *Prayer Response:*

The Bible does not say we have to pray to receive Christ, but many people use that method to affirm a faith response. All Christians should be able to lead their friends into the faith by this means. Pray short and simply . . .

> *Lord Jesus, I believe you are the Son of God who died on the cross for my sins, and rose from the dead. I confess I am sinner who is in need of your forgiveness. I trust in you for the forgiveness of all my sins. Thank you for coming into my life. I commit to follow you from here forward alongside your people. Amen.*

Before leading the response, take these preparatory steps. First, discern readiness for commitment. Second, focus them on praying to Jesus. Make it meaningful! You can say, "These words are for him. There are no enchanted words; it's the expression of faith from a heart wanting to follow, which God receives." Third, have them pray aloud using their own words or lead them phrase-by-phrase, following you verbally. Break it down into bite-size parts, "I believe you are the Son of God." They repeat. Continue through the whole prayer.

Group Exercise:

Break up into groups of two. We want everyone in the group to practice leading each other into the faith. Yes, you need to know how to do this! It is how we communicate with non-believers the substance of the gospel,

 Gathering together

and draw forth from them a response that will give them confidence and security in Christ. This is a critical, foundational part to establishing them as new disciples!

Engagement:

(1) Group Sharing:

- Does anyone have something to share regarding progress with your non-believing friends? Celebrate how God is working! Make sure you take time to pray for God to draw them to himself!

(2) Projects:

- Address whatever is necessary for your projects or outreach events.

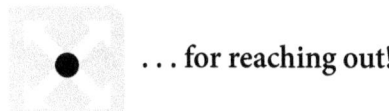 ... for reaching out!

Week #8—BECOME: What Jesus Left Us Co-Missioned to Do!

Please read in preparation for your study:

Without a scholarship, a young man walked on to play football at Long Beach State. As part of the *Pacific Coast Athletic Association*, "The Beach" was a Division 1 football program. Like most conditioning programs of his past, the players bench-pressed three days a week. The notable difference here, however, was that each time this team hit the weights they "maxed"—lifting as much as they could. In fact, there was little rep training. The goal was to get bigger and stronger, and the only way to do that was to lift heavier weights.

Suddenly, he found himself in a distinctly better training environment. In every training session, they yelled and screamed pushing each other to go to higher levels! By the end of the summer, he had gone from bench-pressing a respectable 225 all the way up to 310 pounds! He could barely believe it himself. Nor could his girlfriend. He was receiving the benefit of being in a Division 1 program. It brought measurable results.

Why did this program outperform others? It's because they began with the "end in mind." The coaches knew clearly what the end goal was, and therefore, built a program to achieve the desired result. In this final session, let us sharpen our thinking from the words of Jesus on what precisely he has called us to do. It's time to get crystal clear on Jesus's end goal.

Read Passage: Matthew 28:18–20

> *¹⁸Then Jesus came to them and said, "All authority in heaven and on earth has been given to me. ¹⁹Therefore go and make disciples of all nations, baptizing them in the name of the Father and of the Son and of the Holy Spirit, ²⁰and teaching them to obey everything I have commanded you. And surely I am with you always, to the very end of the age."*

Questions:

1. What specific goal did Jesus charge us to go after?
2. Describe, in living color detail, what precisely we aim to achieve in people's lives?
3. Dialing it in applicationally, what can you do to fulfill Jesus's command with your friend?

 **Gathering together**

Training

This final session deals with the church's discipleship picture. Coming to faith creates a transition to a deeper level of understanding and spiritual growth. Our job is not done when they come to faith! The church exists as a bodybuilding program to develop authentic missional disciples.

To take them into this next level, you must envision the kind of Christian you want them to be. What specific values should they possess? How can you help them become Christ-like in living for God and his mission? According to Jesus, this is the ultimate goal. Please read the principle aloud:

> **Principle:** *It's not about getting a decision, but rather making a disciple.*

If this greater aim is to be reached, time with new believers must be valued. Ongoing discipleship modeling within the small/community group should nurture them in the spiritual life. Clearly, integrating them into your group and church is key! Your pastor must become their pastor. They must become fully part of you, as family.

When it comes to discipling, Jesus blueprinted the relational pattern in how he stayed with the Twelve for three years. After his resurrection, he even hung out with a broader group for forty days. His style of discipleship was personal and ongoing. He was able to produce the movement because they were with him.

 **... for reaching out!**

Additionally, Jesus's method involved both instruction and life-oriented practice. There is always a difference in discipleship when it ventures into action. Can you imagine teaching a child to ride a bike by merely talking about it? No one learns to ride a bike in theory; they have to do it! It's one thing to teach about prayer and another to pray. Teaching about the Bible is good, but giving them an approach to study and then practicing the approach is better. Hearing about authenticity is good, but confessing your sins to another births healing and growth. It is one thing to talk about sharing Christ, and another to learn from engaging in that challenging endeavor.

Remember, people "get it" by doing. We will see higher results if we walk alongside our new believing friends into faith practices. Repetition, reinforcement, and releasing are necessary. Give them an approach, practice it, and then encourage them to act. Make sure you ask how they are doing, provide ongoing coaching, and lovingly hold them accountable where necessary. This is life-oriented discipleship.

Group Exercise:

Break into threes. Discuss amongst the group your experiences of coming alongside others in a nurturing way. Have you discipled before? What have you experienced or learned that is helpful to share?

 **Gathering together**

Further Training Needed...

Please note that every church needs a class or program for newer believers, which can supplement the discipling process that is occurring in your groups. (*Soul Whisperer Ministries* has a potent course called: *First Steps Discipleship Training*, which is foundational for all new believers. And there are additional courses for the progressing stages of growth, as well).

Moreover, be sure to capture on video the efforts of the groups to highlight how God is working! As you build relationships and work at drawing friends in the faith, over the many months and years ahead, please report your stories to church leaders. Also, groups should be intimately involved with baptizing those whom they are discipling. The church is inspired by celebrating the victories of seeing people reached, but also by the engagement of its people in Christ's mission!

Take a moment to review the model.

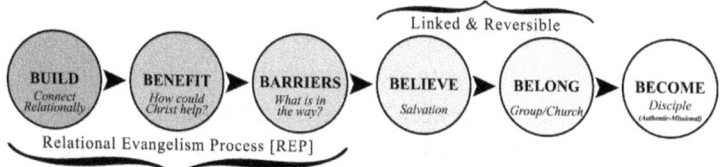

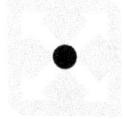   **... for reaching out!**

Build . . .

Building a relationship is the first step. Influence happens through genuine ongoing relationships. When God gives opportunity for a relationship, workers need to realize just how significant that is. A relationship is the bridge to their spiritual journey!

Benefit . . .

The model teaches people to communicate faith's benefits. This is typically the starting point, not the full legal implications of the cross, but rather the beneficial meaning to having faith. Listening carefully to people enables you to see what a relationship with Christ could mean to them personally. It also helps you begin a relevant line of spiritual dialogue.

Barriers . . .

What is holding them back? Do they understand the Christian faith and its "good news" message? Some have important questions to work through. Also, false thinking can snag people, keeping them from following Christ; notions such as, "I could never become a Christian, because I would have to be perfect." Or "God could never forgive me for what I have done." If you help them over these hurdles, they can quickly come to faith. Let's release them from Satan's hellish hooks!

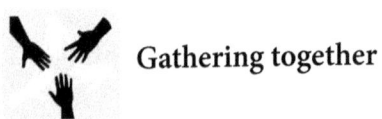 **Gathering together**

Believe . . .

We seek to lead them to an active response—where they put full faith in Christ's death on the cross, repenting of sin, and choosing Jesus. This is a big moment! When a loving relationship is formed and cultivated, and the person's heart is properly prepared, they will come to faith and be baptized.

Belong . . .

They must become part of a church family. Often this happens before they come to Christ, sometimes after. Every Christian belongs in community with others. This is vital to supporting their journey forward. Getting them to a place of feeling connected, and at home in the church is a challenge. It usually takes a consistent effort from believers who genuinely want them to be apart.

Become . . .

What path will undergird their ongoing growth? First, we must journey forward with them relationally. Second, we must invest in their growth through a discipleship process by an individual or class. Remember, the goal is to make authentic missional disciples, where they are walking with Jesus and furthering his cause!

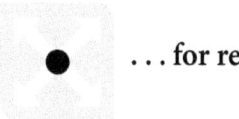 **. . . for reaching out!**

Group Interaction:

Report on and celebrate where you are with building relationships. Let me encourage you to maintain momentum. Don't give up! If you have not completed the project or block party, it's not too late! Follow through, and look for God to show up with your newfound friends!

Congratulations on completing the *Launch Point* mission training! You have made an investment for your growth as a disciple, and toward growing God's kingdom. The tools are laid at your feet. Pick 'em up and use them! May the Lord do amazing works in and through you, as he empowers you to fulfill your part in his heavenly enterprise!

 **Gathering together**

Leader's Notes

From the Author to Group Leaders!

As a Small/Community Group leader, you have an incredible position in your church! Under your pastor's direction, the church is empowering you and your group to fulfill its most essential mission. Your role is super-important!

Humbly, let's admit that it's not typically easy to make new disciples. It takes effort and focus. You will also likely encounter some counterproductive ideas and fear from the way people perceive evangelism. Filling the training gap, you will seek to reframe evangelism into a relational process, and instill a number of exciting new skills! This series is designed to spur your group to interact meaningfully with non-believing friends and community contacts. You will be looking to touch and bless your community! Throughout, be praying for God to show up in big ways!

This *Leader's Guide* will give you some things to think on as you facilitate your group's engagement.

General Facilitating Tips

- The materials break into three complementary sections. You must manage the clock!

- Spend ample, but not too much time on the study/questions part—no more than 10–15 minutes.

- Get familiar with the training section. At times you will want to read it verbatim to be clear. The group must engage ongoingly with non-believers—if you are to see fruit!

- To get the most from the concepts developed in the materials, encourage members to pre-read the session beforehand, if they can.

- Read the principle of each session out loud together. Let it soak in with them for a moment.

- Group exercises are designed to get your people moving with the material. Breaking out into groups of three, allows greater talking and participation!

- The engagement section is there for your practical execution. The group must be working on those areas outside the session as well.

 Gathering together

Input for Sessions

Introduction

In order to prepare your group for embarking on a mission adventure together, take the time to introduce the series. (The introduction could easy be a whole session itself. Recommended). If you choose to go into the first teaching session, then make sure to highlight the overall vision contained therein.

Don't miss the exciting visionary stuff like capturing the Community Group stories on videos, and having people baptize their particular friends! Also take time to look at the model. That is what everyone is going to be learning and doing!

Week #1: The Soul of Mission

Many people have distanced evangelism from Christian discipleship. In this session, we want them to see freshly that being a Christian means being "on mission" like Jesus. Mission is not ancillary, but rather integral to their discipleship and growth.

Before the breakout part, you can disclose your own prayer sentiment as an example. If you make it personally authentic, it will be inspiring!

Week #2: When Faith Is Fantastic

Session two focuses on the faith dynamic with mission. Like all great ventures, faith in what God can do, is a key

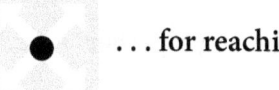 **. . . for reaching out!**

component. In the end, faith is measured by our actions. As you work through the list of names to be praying for at the end, encourage your group to believe God to move—as you step out for him!

Week #3: Learning Faith Formation Process

Understanding process dynamics is one of the most foundational concepts to effective evangelistic mission today. This session will help them to see their participation holistically, and also pares down the process into key stages.

It's not a bad idea to keep identifying friends you will be reaching towards. Build your prayer list! Give them a chance to talk about where they are with relationships at this beginning point.

The breakout, where the group members speak into one another's lives, providing mirroring feedback, can be powerful! Many have never seriously considered what it's like to sit in their circle. Give it ample time. Pray!

Week #4: Getting Real for the Gospel

The authenticity skills taught in this session are counterintuitive to how many view faith sharing. Thinking in rosy idyllic terms, believers can shortsightedly fail to see the influence dynamics within postmodern culture, which values: honesty, transparency and truth above all else! The study session and the chart on Paul's disclosures—demonstrate a biblical basis for communicating openly, and even vulnerably.

 **Gathering together**

Make sure you read the five "Blessings of Disclosure" out loud. It's important for your group to see the many positives that flow out of authentic connecting.

As a leader of your group, you may want to disclose an area of personal darkness, as a case in point to "backdropping" Christ's magnificent light!

Week #5: The Gospel and Its Key

In preparation for this session, please read and reread the training synopsis in order to grasp the concept as well as you possibly can. Remember, this higher-level communication skill takes practice. Although it is not always easy to dig out a key message, the technique is dynamically potent! Make sure you lean into the examples given. This session can excite your group to engage with non-believers! Be praying for God to open their minds and fire their hearts!

When you come to the examples of *gospel key* communication, you can have the group go around and read these out loud. This is the moment when you must assess if the group understands the concept. One illustration that I've used is: "Connecting the dots" between your friends needs and faith in Jesus. Take the time to interact for clarity. Can they fill in the question: If you became a Christian, I see this . . . happening in your life?

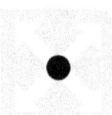 **. . . for reaching out!**

Week #6: Discerning Faith Barriers

Discerning barriers shows you where you need to give attention. It can be tremendously important in guiding conversations.

Note that the study section draws on the knowledge of the group. If your group lacks context with the biblical characters, then you might want to add a little more information.

Also, don't skip the final paragraph that questions if we are the barrier. Sometimes, it's the way we are approaching them that's in the way!

Week #7: Coming Home to Jesus

When I asked a group what would increase their confidence in mission, one man replied rather poignantly, "Actually reaching someone." Helping people make the journey all the way to Jesus is critical for people's salvation, and the excitement of your group! Though, we will undoubtedly not reach all friends and neighbors, we will reach some.

To do so, groups need to provide avenues to call their friends to faith. This session addresses that pivotal, holy transition directly.

Note there are several viable approaches to lead people to Christ. Be sensitive to the Lord on how to go about this. Also be flexible. The critical thing is that we are drawing them into faith and repentance. It might be that you simply lead them to Christ alone in a conversa-

 **Gathering together**

tion. Other times, it's the call to be baptized or take communion as a faith-commitment response.

Week #8: What Jesus Left Us Co-Missioned to Do

The call of God is to make disciples. In the end, every church must look that aim in the eye, and direct its efforts accordingly. Walking forward with people into the faith, church, baptism and community retraces the steps of the New Testament church. Appreciate whose company you have entered!

As a leader, it is critical that you celebrate the efforts, the conversations, prayers, the movement of God's Spirit, relationships formed, the saving commitments and discipleship journeys! Raise the banner for the mission of Jesus in anyway that you can!

Summarizing the model is important to reaffirm the whole process. Again, this training series is intended to launch groups into mission. You may have just begun the trajectory to reach your friends and neighbors. Keep at it, over the weeks and months ahead, and the fruit will come!

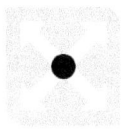   . . . for reaching out!

Addendum

Synergistic Mission through Community Groups

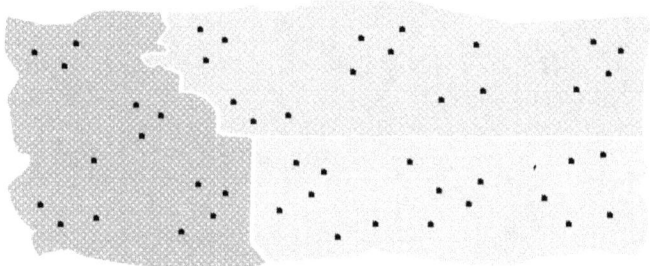

Small Groups versus Community Groups—that's the question. If you desire to move your church into a stronger missional trajectory, rethinking your strategy for groups might be key. Although *Launch Point* is a catalyst vehicle for all small groups, community-based groups do have some favorables. Here's why:

- Region, not affinity, makes "ongoing" connecting easier.
- Neighborhood proximity enhances synergistic efforts.
- Mission-first mindset spurs real discipleship!

Every leader faces the challenge of unseating self-absorbed, ingrown Christians. In the emerging story of Sandals Church, atop of restructuring, we began measuring our people's true missionality: "Change your measurements—change your culture!"

 **Gathering together**

Resources by Gary Comer

Soul Whisperer: Why the Church Must Change the Way It Views Evangelism

This signature work teaches Christians the art of relational influence. Like Jesus, the original soul whisperer, you will learn skills on reading your friends first, to share the gospel at deeper, more resonating levels! Beginning where they are at, *Soul Whisperer* charts how to reach people from their unique starting points.

Steps to Faith: Examine Beliefs, Explore Questions, Encounter God!

In four expandable sessions, this book lays a pathway for spiritual exploration. Short thought-provoking vignettes give seeking people a chance to process, resolve head and heart issues, to eventually place their trust in the Lord Jesus! *Steps to Faith* can be utilized as a class, an interactive group, or a guide for one-to-one evangelistic efforts.

First Steps Discipleship Training: Turning Newer Believers into Missional Disciples

> As Jesus modeled in his post-resurrection appearances, the church must establish new believers in faith, and empower them for mission! This ten-week course instills six essential practices: Bible devotional pattern, conversational prayer, confessional abiding, church involvement, spreading Christ's love and message. The overarching vision is to strategically empower new believers from the get-go!

First Steps Discipleship Training: Leader's Guide

> Rooted in research and proven practice, this Leader's Guide educates in the areas of: Mentoring, Mission, and Methodology. By doing so, it prepares facilitating-leaders to teach a *First Steps* group or class—in such a way—to maximize the disciple making movement or your church.

Elevate: Experience the Power of Lift!

> Building on the discipleship foundation of *First Steps*, this provocative course examines what it truly takes to grow-upward in six key values. Amid the many takeaways, participants will be challenged to go deeper in grace, be more honest about themselves, stronger relationally, increasing in knowledge, mission-engaged, and comprehensive with stewardship.

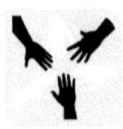 **Gathering together**

Launch Point: Moving Small Groups into Mission

> This mission series is designed to launch small groups into community-based outreach. As groups gather in their neighborhoods, the eight-week course equips members with "process-sensitive" relational evangelism skills. Groups will be led to touch their community through acts of love, and walk alongside others right into the waters of baptism!
>
> Wipf and Stock Publishers: Resource Publications

 **. . . for reaching out!**

www.ingramcontent.com/pod-product-compliance
Lightning Source LLC
Chambersburg PA
CBHW070531100426
42743CB00010B/2041